THE SOBER PHILOSOPHER: WORKBOOK FOR EXPLORING ADDICTION AND CREATING RECOVERY

WORKBOOK

FOR EXPLORING ADDICTION AND CREATING RECOVERY

PEG O'CONNOR

Preface

Dear Fellow Sober Philosophers,

You got this. You are not alone. I am here and I get it.

Thank you for using this workbook. It was designed to complement my book, *Higher and Friendly Powers*. It can also stand on its own. There are additional resources on my website, pegoconnorauthor.com.

We're traveling a similar path, and a strong community helps me to stay on my path. I would love to hear about your journey.

Onward!

Peg
@the soberphilosopher

Contents

Introduction

A question can be an invitation or a judgment. Questions can masquerade as judgments, such as "You're not wearing that, are you?" When encountering that judgment-as-question, most of us will quickly go on the defensive. We've probably had our share of those judgments lobbed in our direction. The questions in this workbook are intended as invitations to explore a subject each of us thinks we know so well—our own selves. When I was drinking, I thought I knew myself completely and none of it was good. I understood myself to be a colossal screw up, a cause of my parents' dismay or disappointment, and a waster of opportunity. I took all of this as unvarnished and hardened fact that could never change. I was wrong on two accounts though. Not all of these were hardened facts and some weren't even true. I didn't completely know myself by being able to list only my transgressions, shortcomings, and failures. That long list merely confirmed my own beliefs about my worthlessness; I couldn't even entertain the possibility that I had positive traits.

I needed to learn more about myself and how other people saw me. I needed to understand why so many of my decisions and actions were self-sabotaging. It was critical to understand what my drinking was doing to and for me. Drinking worked for a short time until it didn't. Even more frightening, I had to accept that there were good things about myself. So much self-knowledge comes from asking questions and giving ourselves permission to answer them truthfully, fully, and free of the harsh inner critic. My challenge is often muting that inner critic who seems only to use her Outside Voice.

The three sections of this book comprise questions and quotations about addiction and recovery from my book, *Higher and Friendly Powers: Transforming Addiction and Suffering*. Each question is meant as a jumping off point for exploration. There are no right or wrong answers; but there may be more or less honest or insightful answers. Some of your answers may straightforward while others may surprise you. To be able to surprise yourself is a gift; it shows that you really don't know everything about yourself. I hope that when you encounter these questions, you hear them in a kind and loving voice. May that same voice be in your answers.

The distance from head and heart to paper and pencil may seem enormous at first, and perhaps for a long time. Putting something on paper seems a commitment that is greater than just thinking about something. Our written words can record our thoughts and feelings, which are exactly what I most feared when I was drinking and trying to stop. I hope you can trust me when I say that as frightening as this is, it can be even more empowering.

There are three sections to this book, each of which has its own short introduction. Most people take things in linear order, moving from the first section, through the second, and to the third. That is certainly one way to use this workbook. There may be value in dipping in and out of the three sections in no particular order. Neither our thinking nor our progress is always linear. Use this workbook in a way that works for you. You get to be the expert on yourself and what you need and want.

Part I

Do I have a problem?

The questions in this section afford an opportunity to explore the history of your using—its effects on yourself and others, and what role alcohol or drugs plays in your life. You will also explore how others see and experience you. It can be a real eye opener when a view of yourself is in sharp contrast to others' views of you. In some ways, these questions are a cost-benefit analysis in which you place each on the opposing plates of the scale. Which plate will be heavier? Your reflections on these questions may result in a much clearer picture emerging. These questions can be answered in any order, and your answers may change even over a short period of time.

QUESTION 1. What was your first experience of drinking or using? How did it make you feel and did you like it?

QUESTION 2. Do you get pleasure from alcohol or drugs that is different from other pleasures?

QUESTION 3. How do you see yourself and where does your alcohol or drug use fit into this picture?

"Inconsistency or lack of congruence in what we want and how we live is a hallmark of addiction. Payment for that inconsistency is always due."

Peg O'Connor
Higher and Friendly Powers

REFLECTION. What are the payments you have made for inconsistencies?

> **QUESTION 4.** What are your hopes for your life? Do alcohol and drugs help you to them? If your hopes and dreams for life have faded, has your use played any part in that?

QUESTION 5. Do you think people expect you to be certain ways and how does your alcohol or drug use intersect with those expectations?

QUESTION 6. Do you find that all your recreation and leisure pursuits involve alcohol or other substances?

"When disappointments, negative experiences, grievances, and aggravations fill one's mind to the point of excluding alternatives, there will always be great suffering. A person may genuinely not care what happens to them."

PEG O'CONNOR

Higher and Friendly Powers

REFLECTION. Are there times when you don't really care what happens to you?

QUESTION 7. Do many people around you drink and use drugs so that you feel a certain pressure to join even if you really don't want to do so?

QUESTION 8. In US culture, drug and alcohol use is equated with fun, happiness, success, glamour etc. Does that seem true for you?

> **QUESTION 9.** Can you make a timeline of your use from the beginning until now?

"When a person realizes she has become exactly
what she promised herself she would never be, she
may face a choice for which she is unprepared. For
example, those who grew up with addicted parents
often promise themselves they'll never become
their parents. When they realize that is what
they've become, they may start to hate themselves
even more. Losing key selves and developing new
hated ones are causes of great shame. That shame
and loss may further accelerate addiction."

PEG O'CONNOR
Higher and Friendly Powers

REFLECTION. What important parts of yourself have you lost? Do you have shameful and new ones instead?

QUESTION 10. Do your family or friends express their worries to you? Does that count as information to you? If they never say anything, does that count as evidence that you don't have a problem?

QUESTION 11. Are there any downsides/bad consequences to your drinking or using drugs? Consequences can be physical and emotional.

QUESTION 12. How do you feel when you are not drinking or using? Do you feel more like yourself? Less like yourself? And what is that self like? Do you like yourself?

"When we do not recognize ourselves in terms of the choices we've made and the actions we've taken, we are often miserable. This misery is a special agony that may provide an opportunity to change."

REFLECTION. Do you not always recognize yourself because of your choices and the present state of your life?

QUESTION 13. Do you ever fib about your use or use secretly in private and then feel guilt or shame about it?

QUESTION 14. Do you ever feel that you deserve to have a drink or use a drug?

QUESTION 15. Do you ever feel like you *need* the alcohol or drugs rather than want them?

"The sickest souls wage wars against themselves.
Their different selves are torn between competing
needs and wants. They live on the dark side of
their misery threshold. They are people who
tend to say No to life and inhabit a world of
grey gloom."

REFLECTION. What are some of the ways you have declared war against yourself? What would count as winning it?

QUESTION 16. Do you see changes in your own behaviors over time? If you do, what were some of the pivotal moments?

> **QUESTION 17.** Could anything else play the same role as alcohol or drugs in your life?

QUESTION 18. Do you struggle to envision a life without alcohol or substances? If you do catch a glimpse of it, what does it look like?

"A person with the worst case of pathological melancholy not only sees no value or worth in himself, but understands there is no worth at all to anything…. A person in the worse throes of it inhabits a fatalism and nihilism that contribute to his inability or unwillingness to try to quit [and]… calls into question whether life is worth living."

PEG O'CONNOR

Higher and Friendly Powers

REFLECTION. At your darkest hour, have you asked yourself whether life is worth living? What would/does make it worth living?

Part II

What can I do to address the problem?

Many of these questions center on identifying what people may need or want in order to change their behaviors and relationships to alcohol, other drugs, and addictive behaviors. Most of us fear the unknown and uncertainty, which may make us stick with what we know rather than take a risk or try something new. The questions aim to help you recognize some resources you may already have or could cultivate. What is each person willing to do to begin to make changes?

QUESTION 19. What kind of support do you think you would need to change your relationship to alcohol or other drugs?

QUESTION 20. Are you the kind of person who won't tell others when you are working on something until it is nearly finished?

QUESTION 21. Are you religious? Spiritual but not religious? How might spirituality fit into your recovery plan?

"The idea of faith presents an obstacle for many
trying to change their addictive behavior....
Faith is not belief in a set of doctrines. It does
not require any certainty. Faith is a willingness to
live on possibilities. To have faith is to act when
the results are uncertain. Acting in the face of
uncertainty may help to bring about certainty.
Moreover, faith runs through all areas of our
lives. Faith can be about anything from mundane
matters to the deeply existential concerns of
people struggling daily with addiction."

PEG O'CONNOR
Higher and Friendly Powers

REFLECTION. Do you have faith in or about anything? Other people or yourself?

QUESTION 22. What is one thing you believed you would never be able to do but did? How were you able to do it?

QUESTION 23. Do you believe you can be the author
or the compelling force in making changes to
your life?

QUESTION 24. Does uncertainty frighten you? Do you have a sense of how much uncertainty you can tolerate?

"Another way [to address] the divine is as the something More to which one stands in a solemn relationship. That something More may include moral principles, patriotism, enthusiasm for mankind, or even better versions of ourselves that we strive toward. All of these conceptions of a higher power/the divine/something More are expansive; they open possibilities and connect us to something bigger than our own conscious selves. They enlarge our lives."

PEG O'CONNOR

Higher and Friendly Powers

REFLECTION. To whom or to what do you want to connect? How might this change you?

QUESTION 25. Why might believing in something bigger than your own present self lessen the sense that you are destined to fail?

QUESTION 26. Have you ever "hitchhiked" on someone else's belief in you?

QUESTION 27. Do you have a sense of how much suffering you can tolerate before you are willing to make a change? Do you think you have reached that point?

"[T]hose without belief in a personified, agential god may still have life altering conversions in which the driving force is some thought, belief, feeling, image, or intuition coming from within themselves."

PEG O'CONNOR
Higher and Friendly Powers

REFLECTION. What is some thought, feeling, or image that gives you incentive to change?

> **QUESTION 28.** Do you struggle with other mental health issues? If so, how do you think they affect your drinking or use?

QUESTION 29. What might change with your family, friends, or employer once you stop using?

QUESTION 30. Do you have family members, friends, or colleagues who have do not drink or use substances? If so, would you be willing to talk to them? What can you imagine yourself saying?

"Acceptance involves activity and agency. Acceptance requires that my actions are responsive to changing realities as well as the recognition that my actions cannot guarantee the outcomes I want. Many external factors are beyond my control. What I can control is my attitude."

Peg O'Connor
Higher and Friendly Powers

> **REFLECTION.** How hard is it for you to identify and then respect the line between what's in your control and what is not? Is it easier to do in some areas of life than others?

QUESTION 31. What are 3 things you would want to know as you undertake the journey to sobriety?

QUESTION 32. Does shame or guilt play a large role in your life? How do you keep them from running the show?

QUESTION 33. Have you started to repair relationships to other people? With yourself?

"Work in recovery—both early and late—
requires coming to recognize the many ways
others confine us and we confine ourselves.
Some of those confines may be very familiar—
they may even be all we have known—and
therefore they are comfortable in a certain
way. Some may even have brought us real
benefit. As we dissolve these confines, we feel
as if we are perceiving new truths even as we
look at old familiar facts."

PEG O'CONNOR
Higher and Friendly Powers

REFLECTION. What are some new truths you've seen as you've looked at old facts during this process?

QUESTION 34. Would you be willing to try a mutual help group such as Alcoholics Anonymous, LifeRing, SMART Recovery either in person or online?

QUESTION 35. Are there major decisions pending in your life? If so, what are they? Is it possible to pause making them until your sobriety feels more solid?

QUESTION 36. If you have a slip or relapse after a period of sobriety, will you think you have utterly failed and all is lost or will you believe you can regain it?

"When we have stopped careening around in zigzag patterns and our impulses no longer have sovereignty over us, then we are much better positioned to take life as it comes to us."

PEG O'CONNOR
Higher and Friendly Powers

REFLECTION. What are 2 or 3 instances where you have felt better able to handle what life throws at you?

Part III

What does sobriety or recovery look like for me?

While recovery most surely involves moving away from troubling consumption, it involves moving toward new ways of coping, relating, working, and loving. These questions help people to get to the business of building better lives where alcohol, drugs, or other behaviors are not central. Living in recovery doesn't inoculate against pain, suffering, and loss. Rather, life in recovery means creating recovery. It isn't something that is merely found or discovered, but rather what each of us generates. Recovery enables us to meet the challenges in healthy and sustainable ways, and makes it possible to become people who feel much more gratitude than grievance. As with the first two parts of this workbook, the questions can be taken in any order and revisited at any time. The final pages are yours to write.

QUESTION 37. Do you feel like you are the same person now as you were when you were using? What stays the same and what changes?

QUESTION 38. What are some of the practical benefits of your being in recovery?

QUESTION 38. What are some of the practical benefits of your being in recovery?

QUESTION 39. What are some of the changes you see in yourself? What changes have other people noticed in you?

"What we need in recovery will change over time, which is why we need to remain nimble and flexible."

Peg O'Connor

Higher and Friendly Powers

REFLECTION. How have your needs changed during this process?

QUESTION 40. Are you more willing to take up space in your own life and not let others make decisions for you?

QUESTION 41. Can you make a list of three goals
you want to achieve for yourself in the next year?

QUESTION 42. What is one surprising thing you have discovered about yourself?

"Expansiveness involves a person extending outward to something More or greater than her previously embattled self. A person may also reach inward to a better self. This expansiveness enables a person to begin to say yes to life."

PEG O'CONNOR
Higher and Friendly Powers

REFLECTION. What are some of the ways you have begun to say yes to life?

> **QUESTION 43.** Are there pieces of yourself you thought you had lost when drinking or using but have reclaimed or rediscovered?

QUESTION 44. Are there issues that feel like unfinished business to you? What will you do about them?

QUESTION 45. Are you better able to accept or make peace with yourself when you make mistakes now? How do you do that?

"As a person expands outward to others
and inward to herself, the loneliness and
isolation that are so common to lives of active
addiction lessen."

PEG O'CONNOR
Higher and Friendly Powers

REFLECTION. Do you feel less lonely and isolated now?

QUESTION 46. What are some of the things you are able to do now that you could not before?

QUESTION 47. If you were always the life of the party when you were drinking or using, do your friends still like and embrace you? Has your circle of friends changed?

QUESTION 48. How do you deal with dynamics or triggers that often led to your use in the past? Do those fade away over time?

"Self-knowledge is not a luxury but rather a necessity."

PEG O'CONNOR
Higher and Friendly Powers

REFLECTION. Can you list 3-5 things you have come to know about yourself? Are any surprising?

QUESTION 49. What are three new coping skills you have developed when you encounter tricky situations?

QUESTION 50. Do you wake up sometimes with a desire to drink or use that feels strong and real? What do you do when this happens?

QUESTION 51. What are 3 things you wished you had known as you started your journey in recovery? Would you share them if you saw a friend struggling in the ways you had?

"Each of us can learn an enormous amount from understanding how others experience us. Where there is divergence in how I see myself and how others see me, that should indicate that something is amiss and requires further examination."

PEG O'CONNOR

Higher and Friendly Powers

REFLECTION. What is one instance where you learned something about yourself from others?

QUESTION 52. Are you able to ask for forgiveness where appropriate and offer yourself self-forgiveness?

QUESTION 53. Do you feel as if you belong to yourself and not to the expectations or opinions of other people?

QUESTION 54. Do you experience more gratitude in life and less grievance?

"Genuine self-forgiveness can help restore
a person's sense that she has moral worth
and dignity even if she has made significant
mistakes and caused great harm to others or
to herself. It all comes down to what she is
willing to do in the present and future."

PEG O'CONNOR
Higher and Friendly Powers

REFLECTION. Are you better able to forgive yourself for making mistakes? If not, what might be holding you back?

9 781961 741003